ILLUSTRATED ANC]
VOLUME TWO
Compiled & Edited by Henry Powers

ISBN: 9781726797399

Entrance to the tombs of the kings of Thebes. Bab-el-Malouk [Bîbân al-Mulûk].

Mosque of Sultan Hassan, from the Great Square of the Rumeyleh

Interior of the mosque of the Sultan El Ghoree [Masjid al-Ghuri].

Dancing girls at Cairo

The coffee shop

The Citadel of Cairo, residence of Mehemet Ali

Tombs of the Memlooks [Mamelukes], Cairo

Modern mansion, showing the arabesque architecture of Cairo.

The letter writer, Cairo

View on the Nile: ferry to Gizeh

Approach of the simoom. Desert of Gizeh

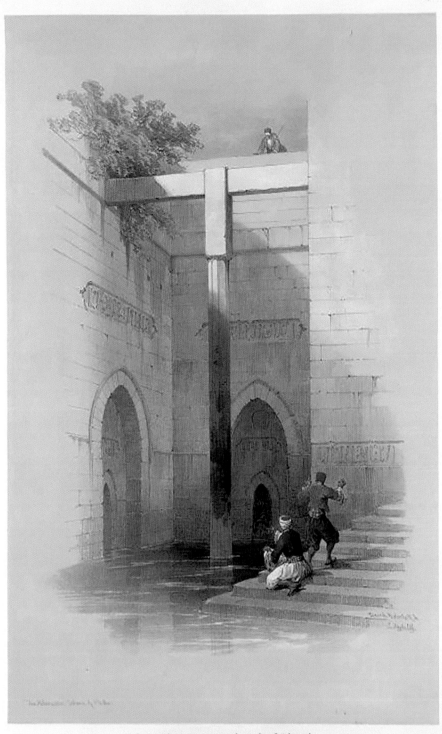

The Nileometer, Island of Rhoda

In the slave market at Cairo

Cairo, from the gate of Citzenib, looking towards the desert of Suez

Bullack, Cairo

Mosque El Mooristan, Cairo

Cairo

Tombs of the Memlooks [Mamelukes], Cairo.

Grand entrance to the Mosque of the Sultan Hassan

Interior of the mosque of the Metwalys [Metwalis]

Minaret of the principal mosque. Siout, Upper Egypt

Bazaar of the coppersmiths, Cairo

Tombs of the Caliphs, Cairo. Mosque of Ayed Bey

The entrance to the Citadel of Cairo

The holy tree of Metereah

Cairo: looking west.

Tombs of the caliphs, Cairo

The minaret of the Mosque El Rhamree

Tombs of the Khalifs [Caliphs], Cairo

Bazaar of the silk mercers, Cairo

One of the tombs of the caliphs, Cairo

Mosque of Sultan Hassan, Cairo

Karnac [Karnak]. Nov. 29th, 1838

Ruined mosques in the desert, west of the Citadel

Minarets and grand entrance of the Metwaleys at Cairo.

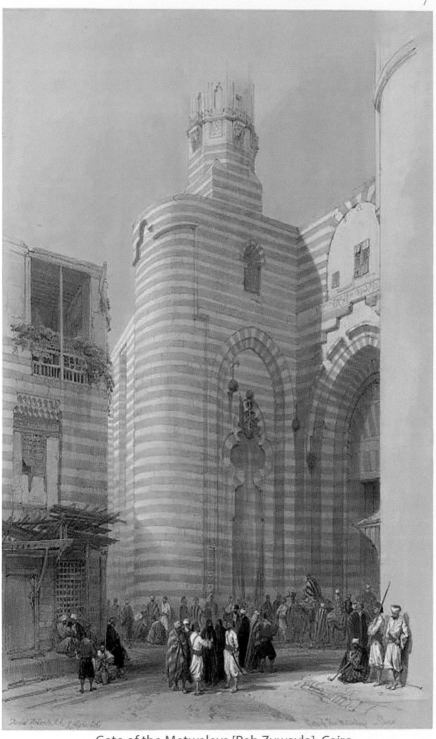

Gate of the Metwaleys [Bab Zuwayla], Cairo

Alexandria

Gate of Victory [Bab an-Nasr], and Mosque of El Hakim.

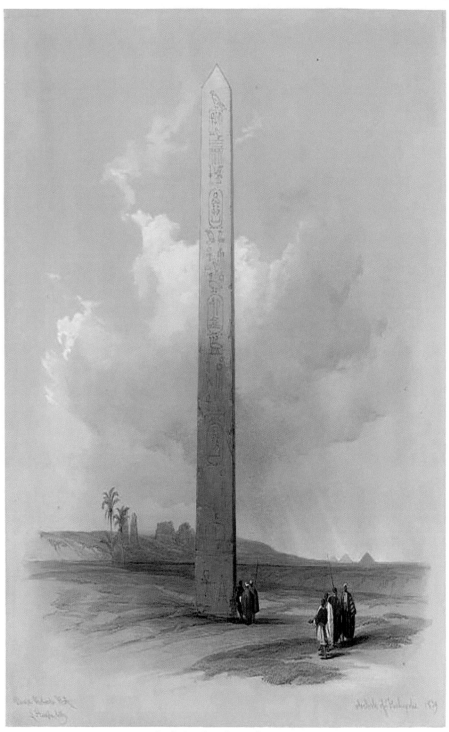

Obelisk of Heliopolis. 1839

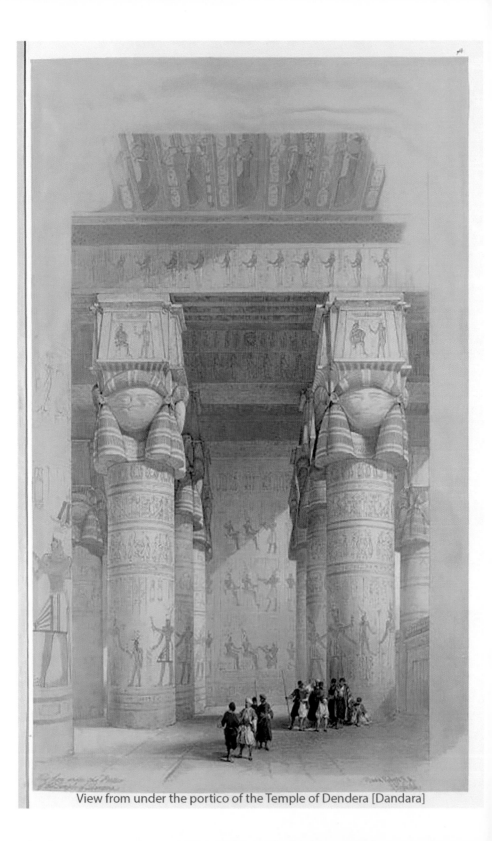

View from under the portico of the Temple of Dendera [Dandara]

Colossus in front of Temple of Wady Saboua [Wadi al-Sabua], Nubia.

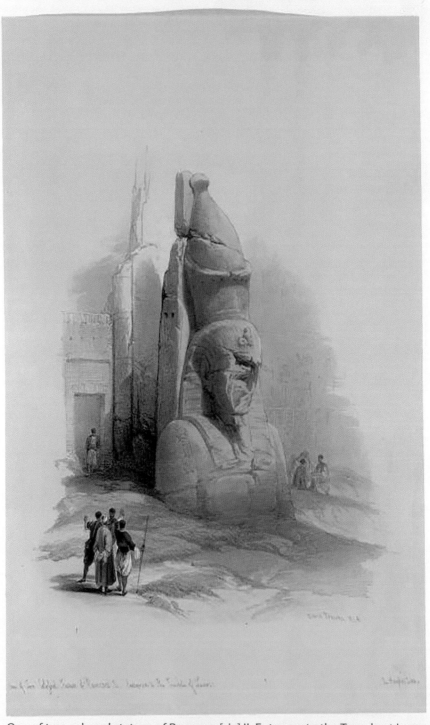

One of two colossal statues of Rameses [sic] II. Entrance to the Temple at Luxor

HIS MAJESTY LOUIS-PHILIPPE, KING OF THE FRENCH.

SIRE,

I solicit, with profound respect, your permission to offer to the world, under the sanction of your Majesty's Name, my "Sketches of EGYPT and NUBIA."

The encouragement which your Majesty has given to the Fine Arts of the enlightened Country of which you, Sire, are the Patriot King, has not been acknowledged in France alone; the Artists of every land gratefully refer to it, as offering, in its proud pre-eminence, the proof that the Arts of Peace can confer a Fame more bright and unsullied than that which is derived from any other source.

Deeply interested in this truth, I have presumed to solicit the honour that my humble name may be associated with such acknowledgment, and that your Majesty will deign to accept this tribute of gratitude from an English Painter.

I am, SIRE,

Your Majesty's most obedient Servant,

DAVID ROBERTS.

Printed in Great Britain
by Amazon